A Director's Guide

Risk Management

HELPING DIRECTORS TO IDENTIFY AND CONTROL BUSINESS RISKS EFFECTIVELY

Editorial Director: Tom Nash
Managing Editor: Lesley Shutte
Production Manager: Lisa Robertson
Design: Halo Design
Commercial Director: Ed Hicks
Managing Director: Andrew Main Wilson
Chairman: George Cox

Published for the Institute of Directors and AXA Insurance
by Director Publications Ltd
116 Pall Mall London SW1Y 5ED
020 7766 8910
www.iod.com

A CIP record for this book is available from the British Library
ISBN 1 901580 99 7
Printed and bound in Great Britain
Price £9.95

Balancing risk and reward

George Cox, Director General, Institute of Directors

The balance between risk and reward is the very essence of business: you have to take risks in order to generate returns. However, there is a difference between risks taken as a result of careful judgement and those taken unwittingly.

In a world of increasing complexity and uncertainty, directors must manage risk more rigorously than ever. Surprisingly many fail to do so, perhaps because they are overwhelmed by the size of the task or because they feel impotent in tackling it. Even more worrying, some remain blissfully unaware of the risks they face.

Every business is surrounded by risks, many of which are both identifiable and manageable. Cashflow and credit management, for example, are two of the greatest causes of business failure when mishandled. Many other risks have grown in recent times: reputational damage, the vulnerability of IT systems to viruses and hackers, and physical threat all figure amongst them.

The need for companies to develop robust risk management strategies is clear. Used effectively, they enable businesses to identify possible threats – legal, financial, environmental, operational – and to introduce systematic plans for mitigation. They also help to reduce costs and insurance premiums.

This guide will help companies develop a practical risk management strategy, which will assist in the day-to-day management of the business. And, if the worst should happen, it also offers advice on damage limitation.

It's all about you

and your business

It is estimated that 80% of businesses affected by a major incident never reopen, or cease trading within 18 months. How can you make sure you are among the 20% equipped to survive if disaster strikes?

At AXA, we are committed to helping you protect your future. Today, that means a clearer focus on risk assessment and management. We have developed not-for-profit products and services designed to help you identify and manage your business risk, and manage your insurance premiums:

- RiskSTOP – providing rapid access to risk management advice and a range of risk reduction products and services
- Risk Assessment Service – a management consultancy service available for detailed risk assessment and management reports and advice
- Risk Management Publications – simple guides to risk assessment, available online at www.axa4business.co.uk

These services are already helping your peers to protect their people, premises and profits. Ensure you do not fall within the 80% danger bracket and contact us today on 0845 3000 678 or visit us at www.axa.co.uk

YOU ONLY HAVE TO AXA

AXA Insurance is the trading name of both:
AXA Insurance UK plc. Registered Office: 107 Cheapside, London EC2V 6DU. Registration England No. 78950
AXA General Insurance Ltd. Registered Office: 107 Cheapside, London EC2V 6DU. Registration England No. 141885
Members of the AXA Group of Companies. AXA Insurance is a member of the General Insurance Standards Council

Taking a systematic approach to risk

Peter Hubbard, Chief Executive, AXA Insurance

Running a business is both exciting and challenging. Every day brings new opportunities and dilemmas, driven by a wide range of factors. The economic climate, changing customer demands and, competitor activity are all amongst the variables that can open new doors or precipitate tough decisions.

From my point of view, successful business management is about identifying, managing and exploiting risk – being ready for opportunities and challenges, and being able to exploit or deal with them before it's too late. Many businesses could reap huge benefits from a more sophisticated approach to risk management.

By taking a systematic approach to identifying, managing and exploiting business risk, many more of the UK's small businesses could build more stable, successful futures. I believe the insurance industry has a significant role to play. Risk management is a core competency for our industry and we have a wealth of risk management skills and expertise at our disposal. At AXA we are working hard to make these skills more accessible to our partners and customers.

This guide is just one example of that. It brings together risk management insights and skills from AXA, the wider insurance industry and beyond and I hope it will contribute to a more profitable future for businesses across the UK.

Chapter 1

What keeps you awake at night?

Businesses and the directors who run them face a multitude of risks. But, keeping these risks at bay and your business safe is probably easier than you think, says Stephen Womack, writer with the Financial Mail on Sunday

EXECUTIVE SUMMARY

- Businesses are now operating in a world full of risk and uncertainty. These risks are constantly evolving and changing.
- Identifying and managing risk is still poorly understood as a business tool. Many failed companies could have survived if they had embraced risk management as central to their business ethos.
- Firms that face up to business risks in a logical and structured way are more likely to survive and thrive.

Who would be a director? Glance at the newspaper headlines in an average week and you will see a long list of threats and dangers to a business.

The business climate is increasingly challenging: new laws and regulations are constantly emerging, threatening to ensnare companies in a morass of red tape. Employees, customers and the general public are becoming more willing to turn to the courts if they feel their 'rights' have been infringed. Maintaining positive cashflow in the face of sluggish payers is a constant battle. Thieves and arsonists are increasingly targeting businesses, where the rewards are high and the likelihood of capture low. Your IT systems might be only one virus-carrying email away from collapse.

And, the world seems to have become a more uncertain place. Climate change has given the UK more windstorms and an increased risk of flooding. Terrorism has taken on new and unpredictable guises. Household-name companies that you might have been trading with for years have collapsed and no-one knows whether company accounts can be trusted anymore.

In the face of such challenges, one understandable reaction is to go 'ostrich like'; stick your head in the sand, concentrate on trying to run your own business and hope to keep out of trouble.

But do you really want to trust your financial future, and that of your company, to luck? The hard reality of business life has shown that even with bucket loads of insurance, companies frequently go under after an unforeseen event, such as a fire or the loss of a key supplier or customer. It is far better to plan to reduce the likelihood of these events and the impact they have if they do occur. Put another way, it is far better to manage the risks.

CATEGORISING RISK

Managing risk means thinking about it in a logical and structured way. Risk to a business can come from within, for example, through the actions of employees, the decisions of management, the choice of accounting policy, the decision to merge or to launch a new product. There are also external threats; risks posed by factors beyond the control of the company or its directors.

It may be more useful to split risk into the following four groups: financial, strategic, operational and hazardous. The table on the page opposite sets out these risks in more detail.

Some risks have traditionally been given greater attention than others. The danger of a factory burning down, for example, is a clear threat to the future of that business. Directors will have considered insurance, invested in alarms and sprinkler systems and had to comply with a raft of health and safety legislation.

Yet more subtle issues, such as overly generous credit terms for customers, lax internal accounting controls or a slight change in the market may contain the seeds of a company's downfall. The biggest cause of business failure in 2001 was lack of cashflow, with the second biggest the impact of bad debts. Both of these risks can, and should, be managed.

TYPICAL DRIVERS OF BUSINESS RISK		
	INTERNAL FACTORS	EXTERNAL FACTORS
Financial risks	Liquidity & cashflow	Interest rates Foreign exchange Credit
Strategic risks	R&D M&A integration	Intellectual capital Competition Customer changes Industry changes Customer demand
Operational risks	Accounting controls IT Systems Recruitment Supply chain	Regulations Culture Board composition
Hazard risks	Employees Properties Public access Products & services	Contracts Natural events Suppliers Environment

Source: The Risk Management Standard 2002 – IRM, Alarm and AIRMIC

THE ONLY CERTAINTY IS CHANGE

Threats to a company are evolving all the time. Legislation changes, new employee rights and new products and technology bring fresh challenges. This means that directors have a duty to constantly monitor the risks they are running – indeed, in this litigious climate, shareholders may take action if they do not.

The Risk Management Standard, published by the Institute of Risk Management and others last year (see chapter 12), sets out a list of duties for directors. It says a board of directors should:

- *know about the most significant risks facing the organisation;*
- *know the possible effects on shareholder value of deviations to expected performance ranges;*
- *ensure appropriate levels of awareness throughout the organisation;*
- *know how the organisation will manage a crisis;*

- *know the importance of stakeholder confidence in the organisation;*
- *know how to manage communications with the investment community, where applicable;*
- *be assured that the risk management process is working effectively;*
- *publish a clear risk management policy covering risk management philosophy and responsibilities of senior management as well as any perceived new risks or failures of existing control measures.*

BOTTOM LINE BENEFITS

But risk control is not just about appeasing the shareholders and ticking boxes on a form. Controlling risks can have tangible benefits to the bottom line. Reducing the number of workplace accidents or industrial illnesses, for example, should lead to a happier, healthier and more productive workforce – and to lower employers' liability insurance costs too.

Likewise, companies that comply fully with the Control of Substances Hazardous to Health (COSHH) regulations will not only stay onside of safety and pollution laws. They may also find that they reduce their use of raw materials, making the production process more efficient. Organisations that fully embrace the disciplines of risk management are frequently better organised, more responsive and more competitive than their peers.

BUILDING A BETTER FUTURE

Thinking logically about risk saved Roxan Construction a lot of heartache and around 15 per cent on its annual insurance bill

The company, based in Southampton, employs 16 staff and turns over around £3m working on building projects along the south coast of England. It develops residential property, runs a portfolio of letting flats and carries out contract repair and maintenance work on behalf of housing associations and local authorities.

BUILDING A BETTER FUTURE

Roxan was prompted into assessing its risk level by its insurance broker Stuart Alexander. The broker put Roxan in touch with Axa's favoured risk management system, devised by Joe Aspey, managing director of consultant Risk Analysis Services.

Paul Fenner, a director of Roxan, says: "We spent about four hours working through a risk survey of the business with our consultant. That led to a report from the consultants with a set of risk management ideas. Over the next ten months, we met once a month to action various risk improvements and set an agenda for the next month."

Roxan ended up implementing around 95 per cent of all the risk management suggestions. Fenner says: "There is now an awareness of risk throughout the business and people are more confident about what they should be doing."

Since completing the process, the company has not suffered any accidents and has dramatically cut the time it takes dealing with the Health and Safety Executive.

Fenner says: "Security has improved and, touch wood, we've seen an end to some problems we had with petty theft," says Fenner. "We were surprised how simple it all was. This is not rocket science."

WHAT IS RISK MANAGEMENT?

Risk management is not difficult. Nor is it some mythical, business school practice, reserved for those with MBAs. We all manage risk every day, from checking for traffic before crossing the road, to locking the office and setting the burglar alarm at the end of the day. It is basic human nature to protect ourselves and those around us.

Most directors, however, could manage risk better. Effective risk management requires directors to understand their business intimately, to ask:

- *How do different operations and processes interact?*
- *What if certain people and/or facilities were unavailable?*
- *How could we operate more effectively?*

Good risk management also requires directors to look beyond the obvious for the dangers to their business. According to the Risk Management Standard, the objective of risk management is:

> *To add maximum sustainable value to all the activities of the organisation. It marshals the understanding of the potential upside and downside of all those factors which can affect the organisation. It increases the probability of success, and reduces both the probability of failure and the uncertainty of achieving the organisation's overall objectives.*

In short, risk management is good management. The following chapters in this guide will explain how to identify the threats and risks facing your business and how to plan and then eliminate, reduce or transfer these risks.

Chapter 2

Be wise to all types of risk

Many small businesses are unaware of those workplace risks that pose the greatest threat to their survival. Mark Cliff, commercial distribution director at AXA Insurance, outlines some simple ways to protect against them

EXECUTIVE SUMMARY

- Integrating risk management into strategic planning and everyday business management can help cut costs and insurance premiums.
- Many businesses do not know the risks they face: 160,000 UK small businesses do not see issues such as damage to premises, employee injury, theft or fraud as threats to business survival.
- In the UK 16,200 businesses are operating without insurance and 210,000 are failing to insure against injury to their employees.
- Eighty per cent of businesses affected by serious incident either never reopen or fail within 18 months.

Every year, thousands of small businesses cease trading due to 'unforeseen circumstances'. In part that is a reflection of market conditions – fierce competition and economic uncertainty mean that running a business has rarely been tougher. But these external issues are really only part of the problem, and many business closures could be easily avoided.

Small businesses are just as likely to fail because they do not do enough to guard against risks such as fire, data loss and injury to employees. Up to 80 per cent of businesses affected by a serious incident of this type either never reopen or close within 18 months.

These threats are very real. They are also predictable and controllable if your board of directors takes risk identification and management seriously.

RELATIVE RISK

Sadly, far too many companies ignore the role of risk management in sound business management. This was borne out by The Relative Risk Report, which was commissioned by AXA Insurance in 2002 and published at the end of the year.

The report aimed to investigate attitudes to risk within the small business community, using a sample of 700 businesses. It examined typical approaches to risk identification and responses to perceived risk through risk management and insurance.

THE THREATS TO BUSINESS

The Relative Risk Report found a marked tendency in small business owner/managers to see business risk as driven by factors beyond their control. Accordingly, the top two threats identified by respondents fell squarely within the 'external issues' category:

- *Nearly 70 per cent of small businesses cited damage to premises as the main threat;*
- *Just over half (52 per cent) of small businesses said illness to key employees would threaten their company's future success.*

Meanwhile, circumstances that can be predicted and controlled were well down the list of priorities for most respondents:

- *Fewer than half identified injury to employees as a significant threat;*
- *Just 40 per cent said inadequate security systems or procedures would represent a threat;*
- *Less than one third (32 per cent) felt that insufficient safety procedures were a threat;*
- *Only 24 per cent saw poor management of premises as a threat to survival.*

These findings demonstrate why so many businesses fall foul of 'unforeseen circumstances'. The tendency to ignore risks that could be controlled means that, inevitably, threats are harder to predict, and the people, premises and profits on which the future of the business depends are much harder to protect.

PROTECT AND SURVIVE

Identifying risks is only part of the solution. Businesses also need to take steps to protect themselves and their employees against them. Many use insurance to protect themselves from external threats; according to The Relative Risk Report, 96 per cent of businesses are insured against damage to premises and 82 per cent against theft or fraud. But, once again, the general attitude towards business protection reveals a dangerous neglect for internal factors:

- *Few small businesses see issues such as inadequate security systems and procedures (52 per cent), insufficient safety practices (33 per cent) and poor premises management (28 per cent) as issues that should be protected against;*
- *Only 87 per cent of small businesses insure themselves against the threat from employee injury, despite the fact that Employers Liability Insurance is a legal requirement.*

These figures highlight a worrying trend. Small businesses are failing to equate poor internal practices with higher risks and, as a result, are not adequately protecting against them.

PLAYING SAFE: INSURANCE COVER

The Relative Risk Report also assessed small business attitudes to insurance and, specifically, whether respondents felt their businesses were over-insured. It found that:

- *Only 16 per cent of businesses felt they were insured over and above the minimum requirement;*
- *More than three-quarters (79 per cent) felt that they were not 'over-insured'.*

It is clear that the majority of businesses still see insurance as a necessary evil – a means of surviving should the worst happen, and not a business tool for minimising and managing risk.

SAFEGUARDING YOUR BUSINESS

One of the most significant obstacles is the misconception that business risk is unpredictable and difficult to protect against. The truth is that many of the incidents that affect businesses are entirely predictable and in many cases preventable.

Business owner/managers have a responsibility to their employees, customers and the general public. They must take action to identify and manage business risk – by making risk assessment and management across the business integral to strategic planning and business management.

Effective risk management is about identifying threats and planning to avoid them. It is not as complicated as it sounds and can help to reduce costs and cut insurance premiums. The following are straightforward steps that any business can take:

Appoint a risk champion

The effectiveness of risk management depends greatly on the competence of the person undertaking assessments and formulating risk reduction plans. Most non-specialist risk assessment should be handled in-house. While it makes sense to appoint a single risk champion to develop a consistent approach based on relevant expertise and training, be sure that risks spanning more than one area of the business are not missed.

Look at all the risks

When assessing risks it is vital that businesses take into account everyone that could be affected by them, including contractors, customers and members of the public. It is important to pay particular attention to vulnerable groups such as young people and expectant mothers.

Be systematic

If risk assessment is to be effective, it must cover every aspect of your company's activities and enable protective measures to be implemented. It should focus primarily on those risks that could affect the company over the long term and identify their most serious potential consequences.

Consult, record and review

Even if you have appointed a risk champion, it is unrealistic to expect one person to be able to identify and assess all risks. Call on specialist expertise from across the business and record and revisit findings regularly. Specialists will identify risks and solutions that a generalist may not, whilst recording and revisiting risk assessments will ensure that progress is measured and solutions are constantly reassessed.

Train your people in safe practices

Ensuring that people are doing their jobs in a safe environment is critical to risk management, but it is only half of the story. It is essential that people are aware of and use safe working practices. Job specific health and safety training and retraining is the only way to ensure that risk management theory works in practice.

Risk Management
Business Continuity
synstar
Sustainable Development
dti
Information Assurance

Chapter 3

Are you a lawbreaker?

How do you keep up with business red tape and ensure that you are operating on the right side of the law? Peter Staddon, head of technical services at the British Insurance Brokers Association, offers some advice

EXECUTIVE SUMMARY

- UK directors have been subjected to a barrage of rules and regulations in the past few years.
- The five core areas of regulation apply to: health and safety, corporate law, finance, the environment and employment
- Trade associations, chambers of commerce and other business groups often give early indicators of rule changes.
- Directors who fail to comply face fines or even a spell in jail.

What does the term lawbreaker say to you? An outlaw, on the run from the posse perhaps? A mugger waiting down a dark alley? Or maybe a burglar, nicking your best silver on a Saturday night?

Unfortunately, today's lawbreaker can just as easily be a respectable director, a stalwart of the local Rotary, who has tripped over some previously unnoticed piece of business legislation and is suddenly on the wrong side of the law.

There has been a spectacular growth in the rules, laws, directives and regulations encircling modern businesses over the past few years. The Federation of Small Businesses lists 27 significant pieces of new business legislation in the past four years alone, with more changes in the pipeline. On top of this there have been hundreds of minor changes to existing rules, revisions of regulations and new guidance.

Some of the changes apply only to certain industries or to particular types of companies; others to virtually every business trading in the UK. Where are the rules coming from? How can directors keep on top of this mountain of red tape? And, what are the risks of not doing so?

CORE CATEGORIES OF REGULATION

Business regulations break down into five main areas:

- *Health and safety – rules to protect your staff and the public from injury and illness.*
- *Corporate law – rules on how your business should be run to allow for an orderly market and to prevent fraud, which can include everything from corporate governance to competition rules.*
- *Financial laws – rules on everything from tax and VAT to the legislation governing listing on the stockmarket.*
- *Environmental law – rules to protect the natural world and to prevent pollution.*
- *Employment law – these rules distinguish who is and is not an employee and define the relationship between a business and its employees.*

UK companies are bound by UK law, but this in turn is increasingly shaped by a series of high-level directives from Brussels that set out common social and business policies across Europe. This European dimension is one reason for the growth in rules and regulations – with more new directives to come (see panel).

Devolution in the UK has also added to the complexity of regulation. Environmental legislation, for example, varies slightly between England and Scotland, so a business operating in both nations has to be sure to comply with the appropriate rules.

In larger companies directors have access to support resources in their fight to keep up with red tape. Accountants and tax advisers are paid, among other things, to keep the firm up to

FORTHCOMING EU DIRECTIVES

- Waste Electrical and Electrical Equipment
- Environmental Liability
- Physical Agents Directive
- Temporary Agency Workers Directive
- Consumer Protection
- Consumer Credit
- Sales Promotion
- Corporate Social Responsibility
- Safety of Services

Source: FSB

date on financial rules and regulation. In many larger organisations there are whole departments devoted specifically to health and safety and HR issues.

Trade associations, chambers of commerce and other business groups can provide some early warning of new rule changes. The best of them lobby government hard to keep the impact of new rules to a minimum. Advisers such as insurance brokers and risk consultants can help on issues including environmental legislation and health and safety guidance.

However, in smaller firms much of the burden of monitoring the rules will inevitably fall on senior management. And the risks of failure are severe. At best, firms can find themselves ensnared in lengthy and expensive investigations by the authorities. Fines and legal action are a possibility. At worst, directors may be disqualified or put in jail.

The Health and Safety Executive, for example, prosecuted 1064 businesses in 2001/2002, with an 84 per cent success rate. The average fine per company was £12,194 – which takes no account of defence costs and the management time involved. It prosecuted 31 individual directors, winning convictions against 23. Five directors have been jailed as a result of HSE action.

Unfortunately, ignorance is no defence. It is the responsibility of all firms, and ultimately their directors, to find out what rules affect them and to make sure they are complying. The evidence is that many are not taking this duty seriously: fewer than one in five managers of SMEs surveyed by the Environment Agency in January 2003 could name a single piece of environmental legislation affecting their firm.

KEEPING ON TOP OF THE RULES

There is no magic formula for staying ahead of red tape but the following common sense tips can help:

- *Make one director or senior manager responsible for monitoring regulation. Include this task in their job description and give them time to do it.*
- *Make regular visits to the websites of relevant authorities. The arrival of the internet has made it much easier to check up on the progress and content of forthcoming legislation (see below). Some bodies, including the British Chambers of Commerce, offer email alert services.*
- *Make use of the DTI Business Link service; its website www.businesslink.org has some pages devoted to regulation, and its local advisers can give more comprehensive help.*
- *Check in with trade bodies. Many have advance notice of which legislation will affect your type of company.*
- *Use your professional advisers such as accountants, insurance brokers and risk consultants. Work with them on an ongoing basis, not just at the time of filing annual accounts or negotiating annual renewals.*

Businesses have blind spots in virtually all areas of legislation. Environmental, employment, and health and safety rules are three areas that have seen huge change over recent years as European

SLIPPERY SLOPE TO NON-COMPLIANCE

Humble heating oil could land a director and his or her company in court. This is the fate in store for those who ignore the Control of Pollution (Oil Storage) (England) Regulations 2001

These are designed to cut down on the number of oil leaks and spills, which account for around one-sixth of all pollution incidents. Yet many companies and their directors are completely in the dark about these recent regulations.

Hairdressers, schools, shops and offices – any commercial premises that stores more than 200 litres of oil outside – are all scooped into the net of this set of rules.

The regulations set out a list of minimum standards for oil storage tanks, pipes, valves and bunds – the containers intended to catch drips or spills. All new installations since March 2002 should have complied. Existing oil tanks in 'significant risk locations', essentially those close to water, must comply by September this year. The rest must be up to scratch by September 2005.

There is no need for an actual oil leak to occur to get into trouble. The Environment Agency can serve enforcement notices on those whose sites are not up to standard and may prosecute thereafter.

Similar rules are in force in Wales & Scotland.

legislation is incorporated into UK law. These are also areas where directors may not always get professional advice. The changes in employment law are so significant that they are discussed separately in chapter 5. Further pointers to help in the other two areas are suggested below.

ENVIRONMENTAL GUIDANCE

Environmental law is produced by the Department of the Environment, Transport and the Regions in England, by the Scottish Executive and by the Welsh Assembly. The legislation is enforced by The Environment Agency – see www.environment-agency.gov.uk and by the Scottish Environment Protection Agency – see www.sepa. org.uk.

However, all of these agencies have joined forces to back NetRegs (www.environment-agency.gov.uk/netregs), a recent initiative aimed specifically at small and mid-sized companies. This excellent website allows users to examine their business stage by stage, to check what, if any, rules apply to their operations.

HEALTH AND SAFETY GUIDANCE

The Health and Safety Executive (HSE) is responsible for implementing and enforcing all health and safety legislation. Its remit runs across the UK.

The HSE website (www.hse.gov.uk) has a weekly 'What's new', which gives a quick glance of new reports, legislation or guidance. It also contains a useful section on consultations, giving an indication of planned new rules and a chance for interested parties to comment. In addition, there is a dedicated small business section.

For those who need to get up to speed quickly, the commercial web service www.hsedirect.com has an online archive of all the HSE publications, plus the detailed legislation: £20 buys a one-day subscription.

The far-reaching Control of Substances Hazardous to Health regulations (COSHH), which were revised last year, control workplace usage of every chemical from plutonium to paint-strippers. Log onto www.coshh-essentials.org.uk for up-to-date information.

Chapter 4

Lowering the risk of litigation

Litigation is almost inevitable in modern business. Deborah Bradley, partner with solicitors Cartwrights Insurance Partners, explains which issues are most likely to lead directors to court, and how to stay ahead of the claimants

EXECUTIVE SUMMARY

- Legal action is increasing, with claims rising in several key areas.
- Companies must think carefully about their relationship with sub-contractors, since liability is not always clear cut.
- Risk assessments should be more than mere paper exercises. Treat every incident as a potential Claim Form in the making and gather evidence accordingly.

Litigation is on the increase. There are new forms of legal expense funding and providers are now chasing custom in supermarkets and through television advertising. In general, the public are more aware of their rights. Both employers and insurers are seen as fair game – the deep pockets that might pay a claim.

PROBLEM AREAS

Businesses are being subjected to a wide range of claims, covering:

- *employer's liability;*
- *public liability;*
- *product liability;*
- *contractual disputes.*

An accident at work can give rise both to a criminal and civil liability. Most employers are aware that they have a duty to provide for the safety of their employees and that they are vicariously liable for their employees' acts. But many do not consider their customers, sub-contractors or cleaners in the same way. As a result, they are caught out by claims arising from the actions of these groups of people over whom, generally, they have less control within their business.

Even, in the employer's liability sphere, more than ten years on from the introduction of the so-called 'six-pack' health and safety regulations, many businesses are not carrying out any – or at least any meaningful – risk assessments.

Going through the motions to produce a risk assessment will not absolve you from responsibility. It is not only a legal requirement that you carry out such assessments, but the process will help you to identify potential problem areas in your dealings with employees, the public and sub-contractors.

SUB-CONTRACTORS

A business's relationship with its sub-contractors is a particularly grey area. Do you owe the same duty of care to provide for the safety of a sub-contractor as you do your own employees? Are you responsible for their acts of negligence? Most directors think that their responsibility to a sub-contractor is not the same as to an employee. They forget that a sub-contractor can, in many circumstances, be deemed to be an employee for the purposes of compliance with health and safety regulations. (The case studies, in the box on page 29, illustrate some common problems.)

The Health & Safety (Miscellaneous) Amendment Regulations 2002 came into force on the 17 September 2002. These regulations aim to clarify health and safety law in areas such as manual handling, protective equipment, first aid, etc. Alongside these, a new guidance note "Use of contractors – a joint responsibility" was published by the Health and Safety Executive. This leaflet is specifically aimed at situations where employers use contractors. It gives guidance on the health and safety responsibilities of employers and contractors to each other, other employees and to the public in general.

WHO'S LIABLE: YOU OR YOUR SUB-CONTRACTOR?

Whether a sub-contractor is deemed an employee or not is not always straightforward to determine

Case 1

A firm of engineers won a substantial contract to fit a heating system in a new factory. It was a busy time of year and its own employees were working to capacity. The firm did not wish to turn the contract down, so it engaged a sub-contractor to undertake the work on its behalf. The firm deliberately paid a generous price for an experienced contractor who had his own business and could work without supervision. He quoted a fixed price. He was walked around the job and discussed the plans with the main contractor. He then had an accident during the course of his work.

Who are the potential defendants?

While the sub-contractor has a duty of care for his own safety and contributory negligence can be alleged against him, the main contractor still has responsibilities for his safety, as can the customer/occupier of the building under the Construction (Design and Management) Regulations. These place an integrated responsibility on various parties involved in a construction project. Where a sub-contractor provides labour-only services, there is always a grey area as to whether he or she might be construed as an employee under the Construction (Health Safety & Welfare) Regulations 1996.

Case 2

Staff training days are commonplace within today's organisations. But many employers do not consider their wider responsibilites to employees and others in such circumstances.

Company A was keen to engender a team spirit among its workers. Employees were booked into a hotel for a weekend and the employer engaged a professional – company B – to undertake training and team-building exercises. The activities were discussed between the two companies beforehand. Directors of company A participated in the sessions alongside other staff.

In one session the staff were split into two teams. The purpose of the exercise was for the team participants to work together to get a huge inflated ball over a net. The game was organised, explained and refereed by company B. In an effort to work together, one member of staff climbed on another's shoulders to gain height and fell.

Was such an accident reasonably foreseeable? Did it arise from a negligent act or breach of duty? If so, is the employer liable or could

WHO'S LIABLE: YOU OR YOUR SUB-CONTRACTOR?

it absolve itself from responsibility by saying that it had placed its trust in a competent independent contractor who had assumed all responsibility for the organisation of the team-building session?

Both the employer and the contractor were sued. It was alleged that, although the contractor had assumed responsibility for the session and had been paid to organise it, company A's directors were present and still retained a responsibility for their staff.

Clearly, whether liability can be proven and, if so, to what extent, will depend on the particular facts of a case. However, any business should look carefully at all activities in which they are engaged to identify potential hazards before they arise.

CAN YOU PLAN THE RISKS OUT?

Risk assessment is the key to avoiding litigation. This applies to all risks, whether to employees, sub-contractors, visitors or to the public. When carrying out risk assessments, ensure that:

- *Hazards are properly identified. You know your business best. The test is whether a risk is reasonably foreseeable. What measures can reasonably be taken to avoid or reduce that risk?*
- *The size of each risk is assessed. Precautions must be proportionate to the potential harm that could arise.*
- *The list of potential hazards is kept up to date, since new working practices will bring about new risks.*
- *Staff are advised of the risks and trained to work safely.*
- *Professional advice is sought.*

ANTICIPATE POTENTIAL PROBLEMS

A continual process of risk assessment should identify potential problems and hopefully avoid them. If an accident does occur, advise your insurer immediately.

Do not just hope for the best and wait for a letter of claim. Delay in reporting an accident is a breach of policy conditions and your insurer may refuse to indemnify if its position has been prejudiced by an inability to investigate the claim at the outset. Other sound practices include:

- *Considering a potential claim at an early stage, while the facts are fresh in witnesses' minds. Gather evidence quickly. This gains an advantage in terms of the litigation process.*
- *Getting a head start and taking advice before the potential claimant does.*
- *Retaining all documents relevant to the accident.*
- *Consulting with your insurers before you implement any changes to working procedures.*

RESPONDING TO A LEGAL CLAIM

How do you react if, after all your best efforts, a legal letter lands on your doormat? Make sure you do the following:

- *Advise your insurance company immediately. If you have reported the accident promptly, they may already have nominated a solicitor to advise you.*
- *If court proceedings are served on you, do not enter a defence yourself. Forward the papers immediately to your insurance company who will appoint a solicitor to deal with the court process on your behalf.*
- *Keep on top of the process. You will only have 14 days from receipt of the papers for your solicitor to enter an acknowledgement of service. Time is of the essence if you wish to avoid a default judgement being entered against your company.*

Chapter 5

Could employees be a liability?

Employees have more legal rights than ever before. Nic Paton, business journalist, explains how directors can minimise the risks of infringing these rights, and ensure that they have a healthy and productive workforce

EXECUTIVE SUMMARY

- New laws on religion, disability, sexual orientation and age mean employers run greater risks of workplace discrimination.
- Managers cannot afford to avoid workplace bullying. Employers need to have a clear policy and implement it.
- Industrial illness must be managed and firms should take a pro-active stance with rehabilitation for injured workers.

Compensation is one word most directors dread hearing from their staff. According to the TUC, compensation payments to employees now total more than £2bn a year. Employers complain they are drowning under a sea of employment legislation, a situation compounded by often frivolous or malicious personal injury claims by employees.

Workers now have more rights than ever, and are more likely to bring a tribunal action or court case. Yet, at the same time, employers have more responsibilities to their staff than in the past.

If directors want to manage their business risk effectively in relation to their employees, and avoid being faced with a hefty compensation bill, they need to focus on three main areas:

- *discrimination*
- *workplace bullying*
- *industrial illness.*

DISCRIMINATION

Sex, sexual orientation and religion

Draft regulations concerning protection from discrimination on the grounds of sexual orientation and religion were introduced by the government in 2002 and are expected to become law by the end of 2003.

These will put religion and sexual orientation on a par with gender and race as areas where workplace discrimination on pay – or any other grounds – is strictly taboo.

Employment lawyers have predicted the laws could result in a huge increase in discrimination and harassment claims, with offensive office banter, emails and the working environment all likely areas of dispute.

Directors will also need to be wary of continuing worries about the gender pay gap, which last year led to a number of high-profile court cases.

On the religious side, lawyers foresee a raft of claims relating to time off for religious observances.

Age

Regulations to outlaw age discrimination are due to come into force in 2006. In late 2002 the government upped the ante on the debate by proposing to scrap the compulsory retirement age.

Both of these proposals represent potential minefields for employers, who will have to ensure they are not retiring people unnecessarily or, conversely, making them work reluctantly into old age. Furthermore, employers will have to be careful not to put frailer older workers at risk of injury.

Disability

Under the Disability Discrimination Act of 1995 (DDA), it is now the duty of an employer to make reasonable adjustments to the workplace so that a disabled person can be employed.

At present, the DDA only covers employers with more than 15 staff, but this is expected to change from October 2004, when the small employers' exemption is scrapped.

The key to managing all the new discrimination regulation, says Dianah Worman, an adviser with the Chartered Institute of Personnel and Development (CIPD), is not to take it personally. Frustrating as they may seem, these laws are all about assisting businesses to recognise that maybe they are not helping themselves if they make judgements about people, she suggests.

Also, change can only be effective if it is pushed from the top. A half-hearted director will, at best, effect only half-hearted change. The best advice is to:

- *Instruct those responsible for equal opportunities policies to ensure that they are not mere paper promises, but have real meaning and effect in the workplace.*
- *Take a close look at your recruitment and promotional activity. Are you making it hard for applicants to comply with traditional dress codes, for instance?*
- *Train all employees, and especially line managers, in recognising the importance of non-discriminatory behaviour and how to raise complaints.*
- *Appoint harassment counsellors to act as informal sources of advice.*
- *Deal firmly, but proportionally, with offenders.*

WORKPLACE BULLYING

Workplace bullying is shooting up the business risk agenda. In 2002, a study by the journal IRS Employment Review found that more than one in three organisations have experienced unresolved staff complaints leading to employment tribunal claims in the past three years.

And, according to Mercer Human Resource Consulting, more than one in five employees was bullied at work at least once during last year.

Under last year's Employment Act, which came into force in April 2003, employers are now legally obliged to act when an individual raises a bullying or harassment complaint. In addition,

STAMPING OUT BULLYING AND HARASSMENT

In 2002, the postal services firm Consignia was described as suffering from a culture of bullying and harassment in an independent report on its industrial relations

Trade union Amicus, meanwhile, estimated that bullying and harassment cost the firm about £15m a year. To top it all, the company was forced to admit that racial abuse had led to Jermaine Lee, a young black postman, killing himself. After Lee's family won the right to take Consignia to an employment tribunal, the company settled out of court.

To its credit, Consignia responded with a huge internal investigation and overhaul of procedures in an attempt to stop further bullying. Initiatives included a complaints procedure that put the HR department at the centre of solving disputes rather than local management. From April 2003 staff have also had access to a harassment phone line where they can get advice without having to go through managers, and investigators from other departments are employed to probe any complaints.

Complaints must be resolved within a given timeframe, otherwise they are passed on to a higher level. Training in handling bullying and harassment has also been included in staff induction sessions.

a basic statutory grievance procedure must be written into all individual staff contracts.

Spotting bullying and harassment requires thinking ahead and, when there is a problem, being firm, fair and transparent.

On a practical level, it is advisable to:

- *Put strategies in place to govern how assaults on staff are reacted to and how your organisation responds to concerns.*
- *Assess any risks for employee health and safety, particularly when workers are dealing with members of the public.*
- *Show support for your employee and be prepared to call the police if the harassment or bullying is coming from a member of the public.*
- *Have a clear disciplinary code for dealing with bullying and harassment by colleagues. When a complaint is made, hold an investigation and be seen to be fair.*

INDUSTRIAL ILLNESS

While workplace deaths and serious injuries are decreasing, absence due to illness or injury remains a major problem, according to the Health and Safety Executive (HSE). It estimates that 40.2m sick days were taken last year. Cases involving stress and musculoskeletal conditions, such as repetitive strain injury (RSI), are burgeoning. If employers mishandle such absences they risk ending up in court.

The CIPD estimates sickness absence costs the UK economy some £13bn a year. Stress, it found, is the most common cause of long-term absence for non-manual workers. The institute has published a guide on helping employers manage stress in the workplace, which can be obtained through its website www.cipd.co.uk.

DON'T LET STRESS EAT YOU UP

Rising absence rates at crispbread manufacturer Ryvita began ringing alarm bells for managers last summer. An audit revealed that increased stress was causing an absence rate of six per cent among the 300 staff based at Poole, Dorset, compared with the four per cent average elsewhere in the company

Ryvita turned to consultant Right Corecare, which drew up an employee assistance programme at a cost of £20 per employee per year. The programme gives employees access to a helpline offering advice and information on stress, anxiety and depression. Staff can also get legal and financial advice; both are areas that often contribute to stress.

Beyond this, if employees are found to be getting into difficulty, they are entitled to six counselling sessions, with the first one taking place within five days of the problem being spotted.

A series of one-day training courses for line managers was also arranged to help them to spot signs of stress — both in themselves and their employees – and to identify best ways of tackling it swiftly.

The company plans to carry out a formal audit this summer to see what effect there has been on absence rates, but anecdotal evidence already indicates it is a popular and effective initiative. "So far the feedback has been very good. People are using it and say that it has been extremely positive for them," says HR manager Heather Palmer.

The IoD has also published a Director's Guide to managing health, safety and wellbeing at work, which gives clear advice on how to identify and tackle key issues (see www.iod.com).

The HSE intends to introduce management standards on stress by the end of this year. Employers will be able to use these to judge whether their organisation is suffering from stress.

Organisations should:

- *Ensure line managers are adequately trained in how to spot stress and other health and safety issues before they become a problem.*
- *Conduct regular workplace risk assessments, adjusting workplace processes if necessary, and carrying out internal stress audits, perhaps using an online or paper questionnaire.*
- *Introduce pre-employment health screening.*

REHABILITATION

Retraining and rehabilitation are absolutely critical parts of the business risk management process. Yet, they are often overlooked by employers.

Research by the Work Foundation has found that while the majority of employers do have written policies on rehabilitation they are often hamstrung by the attitudes of line managers, the limited capacity of the NHS and resistance from employees.

Diane Sinclair, a CIPD adviser, says that one of the problems can be that managers are frightened to act when someone is on long-term sick leave. Such anxieties need to be overcome, she stresses, since contact with the employee is absolutely vital.

In stress cases it's vital to look at the person's working environment, the organisation's culture or the management style.

Many employers benefit from calling in the services of an occupational health (OH) specialist who can put in place appropriate preventative measures, training and rehabilitation schemes. There is no central register of OH nurses in the UK, but your company GP will normally know of local OH providers. Otherwise, the Association of Occupational Health Nurse Practitioners keeps a voluntary register, as does the Royal College of Nursing.

EMPLOYERS' LIABILITY INSURANCE

As well as being good for your business, morale and workforce, cutting down on accidents and compensation claims can work wonders for your relationship with your employer liability insurer.

The increasingly litigious workforce has led to a hike in premiums for employers' liability insurance. The Engineering Employers' Federation estimates premiums have risen by 400 per cent and the Association of British Insurers calculates the increase at 100 per cent over five years.

These worries prompted the Office of Fair Trading to launch a fact-finding study into the UK liability insurance market in late 2002, with the prospect of further investigations if anti-competitive behaviour was discovered.

Chapter 6

Time to get personal

The rewards of being a director are great, but so too are the personal risks directors face in doing their job, says Natasha Muktarsingh, Enterprise Editor of the Financial Mail on Sunday

EXECUTIVE SUMMARY

- Directors can be held personally liable for the failings of their firms, risking disqualification, fines and imprisonment.
- Directors' health often suffers through work, with stress a growing problem. Don't overlook this; admitting that you need help is not a sign of weakness.
- Death or illness of a director can be highly damaging to a business.
- Insurance and good management techniques can control some of the risks.

In the cosy world of the employee, the risks faced by those running the company seem few. Many perceive directors as being there to make grand plans and to take a grand salary in return for their limited pains.

But stepping into the role of company director brings with it numerous personal liabilities that, if ignored, could bring about a director's financial, not to mention emotional, ruin.

Directors are often amazed to learn just what they can be held personally responsible for. To start with, there are a number of general liabilities that come with running a company:

- *Directors can be pursued by the company itself for breach of duty, breach of trust or negligence. They can be taken to court for any losses suffered by a company as a result.*

- *Personal liabilities can also occur when the director causes losses to any of the stakeholders in a business as a result of negligence.*
- *Regulating authorities may also find a director in breach of criminal or civil law because he is a director and, therefore, in control of the company.*
- *As chapter 3 explains, directors can be prosecuted under rules governing health and safety and consumer protection. An individual, as well as a company, can be held responsible for the death or injury of an employee or member of the public.*

INSOLVENCY

Where a company collapses, a director can be prosecuted in two specific circumstances:

- *If the liquidator finds that a director intended to defraud or knew the business was being carried on with the intention of defrauding creditors.*
- *If the liquidator decides that the director knew or should have known that the company was likely to go bust and did not take all reasonable steps to minimise the loss to creditors.*

In such cases, the amount the director is penalised for is decided by the court. Some measure personal liability by looking at how much of the company's assets have been lost since the time the director should have realised that liquidation was inevitable. There is also a Forensic Insolvency Recovery Service, run with The Insolvency Service by a group of private-sector insolvency specialists, that will take legal action against directors in appropriate cases.

DISQUALIFICATION

Directors can be disqualified if they are found guilty of an offence under the Companies Act, if:

- *they persistently fail to comply with the Act's requirements for filing information; or*

- *they are a director of an insolvent company.*

If a court rules that a director of an insolvent company is unfit to have a management role, he or she may be prevented from holding a management position for a minimum of two years and a maximum of 15 years.

The DTI polices director investigations and has stepped up its enquiries in this area over the last few years. In 2000 alone, there were around double the number of directors disqualified compared with the first ten years of the legislation. Other government bodies, such as the Office of Fair Trading, can also call for a director to be disqualified.

Directors need to know all the risks their particular company faces and what impact that can have on them as individuals. Directors and Officers' insurance can go some way to cover them against these liabilities. However, an increase in claims of this type has driven up the cost of cover and is making it more difficult to obtain.

Directors considering liability cover should make sure they are covered both as individuals and as part of the board as a whole. A director who is also professionally qualified – as a chartered accountant, for example – can also take out professional indemnity insurance to cover himself further.

LOSING A KEY MEMBER OF THE TEAM

There are also human risks that need to be recognised by directors and their boards. No-one is immortal or accident proof, yet all too often directors ignore the possibility of their colleagues or themselves being unable to work and the impact that this could have on the company. Many businesses have no succession plans in the event of a key member becoming incapacitated.

If a fellow director or key executive is taken ill or dies they could take with them essential intellectual capital, as well as business contacts, potential contracts and customers. As a result, the company could suffer financially, even facing bankruptcy, and individual directors would suffer.

In the event that a director dies, his or her stake in the business could pass to a spouse or another nominated person. The board may find that this spouse wants to sell their stake in the business to a rival or take some claim on the business as a major shareholder.

Alongside a formal contingency plan, key man cover is one way to help protect against this kind of incident. An insurance policy covering a key person can help pay for finding and training a temporary or permanent replacement. Adequate insurance can also provide the capital for fellow directors to buy back the shares of a deceased director.

IS RUNNING A BUSINESS A RISK TO YOUR HEALTH?

For most directors the risk of being taken to court for breaking the rules is remote. A far more common risk, but one often overlooked, is that to their personal health. Most directorships demand long hours, heavy workloads and little time for relaxation. The result is frequently stressed out, unhealthy executives.

Increases in employee liability claims are forcing employers to acknowledge the existence of stress in the workplace. But most see the admission of it at executive level as something of a weakness. Stress affects different people in different ways, but if left untreated for too long it can undermine a director's health and ability to do their job.

According to research conducted recently by Axa Insurance and the International Stress Management Association, nearly two thirds of all owner-managers who set up their businesses to escape the stress of corporate life were just as stressed – or more so – as they were in their previous jobs.

The study discovered that all young directors between the ages of 18 and 24 felt more stress than they had as an employee and 60 per cent of 55-64 year-olds were also suffering more after they set up their own companies.

When directors become stressed by running their own businesses it impacts on others: the research also found that 42 per cent of staff working in small businesses blamed the stress they

STRESS PUTS STRAIN ON NEW VENTURE

When Dan Jackson set up in business his optimism about being his own boss soon dissolved in the face of mounting pressure to succeed

Two years ago, while working as a sales executive for Capital Radio, Dan Jackson had an inspired idea to help firms create a brand using sound. Jackson left the station and set up his own firm called SonicBrand, but a year into his new role he found himself on the edge of a nervous breakdown. He says: "No-one expects their business to struggle or to be poor. I saw setting up my own company as a way of being my own boss and making money, but I soon realised it was not going to be as easy as I thought."

Jackson found himself disappointed and worried when supposed sure-fire pitches to potential clients were turned down. He had invested all his savings in the business and was being supported financially by his wife. "The financial problem was a real focus of the stress I felt," he says. "Everyone warned me how hard it would be but I was fuelled by optimism. Actually running my own business was a rude awakening – you do not get any time away from it."

As the stress began to take over, Jackson realised he had to act quickly and turned to his business partner and his wife for help. Sharing his problems helped him get on top of the situation and he took steps to minimise the risk of getting into the same trouble again. These steps included staying open about his fears for the company, moderating his lifestyle and taking regular exercise. SonicBrand also has indemnity insurance for the business and a company health insurance scheme.

felt on aggressive management and poor communication. So, stress at work not only means unhappy individuals but bad business too. A company director has a responsibility to keep him or herself in good health and set that standard for the firm's employees.

Many employers are offering counselling services for stressed staff, gym memberships and health screening as ways of keeping on top of the problem. David Williams, casualty insurance manager at Axa, says: "Directors are key to a company and cannot afford to be lost to something like stress.

"If you find problems at an early enough stage, you can generally do something about them. Health screening and regular testing is one way of doing this."

Chapter 7

Protecting your physical assets

Insurance can pick up some of the bills if your business burns down or ends up under water. But prevention of a disaster is far better than the cure, says Mike Butler, risk control strategy manager at AXA Insurance

EXECUTIVE SUMMARY

- Flood and fire are the main hazards to tangible assets.
- Reducing risk to buildings and equipment starts at the design stage. Use the wealth of expert advice available.
- Good working practices help cut risks further.
- Beware of the risks caused by third-party contractors.

A company's buildings, plant and equipment are its most tangible assets. So it is surprising that many directors have a blind spot when it comes to managing and reducing the risks of damage or destruction to these key resources.

The physical elements of your business are exposed to a multitude of risks occurring both inside and outside the company. There are many causes of loss that are likely to affect a business but the major ones, based on the experience of insurers, are:

- *Fire – caused potentially by:*
  - *arson;*
  - *an electrical fault;*
  - *smoking;*
  - *process work;*
  - *the actions of third-party contractors.*

- *Flood and storm.*
- *Subsidence.*

You will notice that external forces represent two of the main causes of fire. Although these are not directly part of the business, this does not mean that they cannot be controlled. (The threats to business from crime are discussed more fully in chapter 8.)

RISK ASSESSMENT

When a business has become aware of the risks it is exposed to, the process of risk reduction becomes easier. To evaluate exposure, you need to carry out a formal review and risk assessment. There are many risk assessment models available and insurers themselves use a variety of tools to assist this. (Chapter 10 explains the process of risk assessment more fully.)

Risk assessment is now the accepted method used by regulatory bodies such as Health and Safety Executive and the Fire Brigade, for identifying and dealing with the greater risks.

DESIGNING OUT RISK

When constructing new or extending/refurbishing buildings it is important to remember that the Building Regulations and Building Standards are the minimum acceptable standard. They are driven by the need to protect life, not your business.

Modern building techniques mean that traditional bricks and mortar are now used far less frequently. Modern alternatives are lighter, cheaper and provide better thermal insulation. They do, however, present the building owner with the new problem of understanding how this might affect the risk to the business.

The insurance industry, in conjunction with the Building Research Establishment (BRE) and Fire Protection Association (FPA), has produced an acclaimed publication called *The Design Guide for the Fire Protection of Buildings.* The guide has been prepared to enable architects and designers to take into account business risk management issues in relation to the fire protection of buildings. The *Design Guide* should be used in conjunction

BAPTISM BY FIRE

Changing business needs can transform completely the risks that a company faces. One food-processing company was ravaged by fire, having changed the physical structure of its factory, but not its risk assessment intelligence

The company had been trading successfully for many years in a traditional building constructed from brick. Changes to environmental health regulations required the business to improve the internal process and storage areas by creating a 'food safe' structure within the factory, using 'wipe clean' insulated panels.

The panels comprised two thin sheets of metal with a core consisting of a combustible insulation material and were simply jointed together to form rooms within the original building.

Later, a contractor was employed to fit a safety handrail to an elevated platform. During welding a spark ignited the combustible core within an adjacent panel. The fire spread rapidly through the combustible insulation within the panels, causing the internal structure to collapse. The building was completely destroyed.

This example gives us key learning points:

- Understand the risks associated with modern building materials. Whenever the business makes changes, re-evaluate overall risks.
- Consult with insurers when undertaking changes to your business premises – they may be able to assist in the specification of appropriate materials.
- Understand and control the risks posed to your business by third-party contractors – hot-work permits can be used to control contractors.

with the documents supporting building regulations and should be regarded as being of equal importance.

As well as assessing risks relating to physical construction, it is important to evaluate the external environment of the building. This will include the control of hazards presented by waste, stock, vehicles and fire-water supply. External landscaping can also assist in reducing the exposure to the threat of arson, theft and exposure to flood damage.

Using design to minimise risk does not stop with construction and layout. It is important to consider the provision of effective fire protection, such as devices to prevent the spread of fire between floors/compartments, automatic fire alarms and sprinkler installations. Fitting these at construction stage will be more cost-effective then retro-installation. And, the incorporation of certain fire protection systems, to insurers' standards is often rewarded by premium reductions.

FLOOD RISKS RISING

In recent years, the incidents of flooding have increased owing to the rising rainfall levels in the winter months and the ongoing effects of global warming.

With no sign of this abating, what can directors do to protect themselves? The simplest precaution is to consider carefully the location of your business and establish if there is a significant risk of flooding. This will, of course, be a primary consideration for new properties.

Even properties in high-flood risk areas are benefiting from engineered solutions, which can be as simple as landscaping to direct waters away from your premises. Don't forget that even if your building is not flooded, if nearby roads are impassable then your employees will not be able to get to work and your clients may find deliveries are interrupted.

Your business risk assessment should not just relate to river and/or coastal flooding risk. Many towns and cities have Victorian sewerage systems that are incapable of coping with rainwater run-off, due to the population changes.

For many businesses relocating is impractical. If you are in an area susceptible to flooding, it is important to be prepared. Consider the following measures:

- *Time is critical so draw up a flood plan that can be brought into play if flooding is threatened. This should include:*
  - *consultation with The Environment Agency through Floodline;*

- *notification procedures for staff and customers;*
- *initiation of loss reduction measures.*

- *Physical protection products: barriers, seals, drain valves and air-vent covers that can delay or prevent water seeping into a building. A publicly available specification for anti-flood devices has just been introduced by the British Standards Institute.*
- *Think about where high-value stock, plant and vehicles are kept. Can they be relocated rapidly?*
- *Key utilities should be designed and located to ensure that minimal damage is sustained in the event of flood occurring, eg. electrical switchgear, compressors, generators, IT and communication servers.*
- *Businesses that use or store chemicals should assess the likely impact of possible environmental damage and prosecution in the event of the chemical escaping into a watercourse or the area surrounding the premises.*

WHERE CAN I GET HELP?

There are many sources of authoritative information including the Fire Protection Association (FPA), the Arson Prevention Bureau, the Environment Agency and the Scottish Environment Protection Agency. Contact details for these and many other organisations are listed in the further information section.

The majority of insurers understand that loss prevention makes sound financial sense. They employee specialist field staff to visit business premises and to provide sound risk management advice to assist the business. Similarly, many insurance brokers are aware of the importance of risk management in modern business and employ their own staff to provide guidance on a range of business protection issues.

Regulatory bodies such as the local Fire Brigade, Health and Safety Executive and Local Authority licensing authorities provide free, independent advice and guidance.

Chapter 8

The high cost of crime

Crime costs the average business around £5,000 each year, not to mention hours of wasted management time. Stephen Womack, writer with the Financial Mail on Sunday, explains where to start in the fight against crime

EXECUTIVE SUMMARY

- Businesses cannot afford to ignore crime. They need to record and report it to understand the true costs.
- Safeguarding the workplace is the first priority. Some risks can be designed out, while others can be managed.
- Co-operation with other businesses and local authorities is the key to managing some of the bigger risks.
- Electronic crime is proliferating; the risks from your own employees should not be underestimated.

Measuring the number of crimes against business is not a simple process. Most police forces record crime by type of offence, not by type of victim, which means that separating out business crime is not always possible.

However, independent research suggests that all too often a business is the victim. One study by Liverpool University on crime in Merseyside found that small business premises were eight times more likely than homes to be burgled in any one year.

The British Chambers of Commerce Business Crime Survey 2001 put the annual cost of crime against firms at £19bn – that's roughly £5,000 per year for every business in the UK. One firm in ten reported that crime was costing them more than £10,000 each year.

On top of the direct costs of vandalism, break-ins, arsons or assaults, crime harms a business because it can:

- *disrupt trading;*
- *lower staff morale;*
- *damage a company's image.*

Left unchecked, crime can also raise insurance costs or make some types of cover difficult to obtain. And, in the worst affected areas, crime can make it hard to recruit new staff or even force firms to move to a new location.

While no company is immune to crime, the risks will vary depending on your business activity and your geographical location. Every director needs to be aware of the threat of crime, no matter what the firm's past experience. Directors also need to understand that these risks can change over time.

BE OPEN ABOUT CRIME

You can only control a problem if you understand it and face up to it. This means recording and reporting all crimes or attempted crimes that affect a business.

A company security register or security diary should always be maintained. If details of incidents are recorded, including every associated cost, these can be analysed at a later date to discover trends and identify the most effective preventive action.

Some firms neglect to report minor crimes to the police; they expect little by way of response and worry that insurance costs will rise if they present a full dossier of these events at renewal. But this is blinkered thinking. Police can only respond to what they know about and reporting crime fully will give them better information to spot patterns of activity and to prevent future problems.

SAFEGUARDING THE WORKPLACE

Crimes within the workplace – theft, arson vandalism, etc. – are the most obvious dangers facing most businesses. Many firms will have taken some basic crime prevention measures, such as fitting alarms or security grills. But there is always scope to do more.

Each firm will face its own risks. However, some general crime reduction tips include:

- *Take security advice: insurance companies and brokers, local authorities and the police will all give free advice on crime prevention.*
- *Don't shout about what you've got. Does a warehouse have to be signed 'XYZ Sports Goods Ltd', for example?*
- *Think about rubbish. This can be used both as fuel for an arson attack and as a potential source of information about your business. Lock bins to posts away from your building to reduce the damage if someone does set it alight. Consider secure disposal options for sensitive waste.*
- *Seek expert advice before investing in sophisticated and costly equipment such as anti-arson letter boxes, CCTV or smoke generators. They can help deter crime but you need to be sure that the benefits will outweigh the costs.*
- *Also think twice before fitting razor wire, spikes, etc. to walls and fences. Perversely, you owe a duty of care even to trespassers, who could be entitled to sue if they were to be injured.*
- *Record and store securely serial numbers of all equipment. This can aid recovery of property and be vital evidence in prosecuting thieves and those trading stolen goods.*
- *Join forces with other local businesses for more ambitious projects (see section on page 53 on working together).*

The risk of some crimes can be reduced through smart design of buildings, car parks and access roads. This particularly applies when a firm is building from scratch in a new location, but some aspects of secure design can also be incorporated later.

The Association of Chief Police Officers runs the Secured by Design scheme, covering both design and security products. Log on to www.securedbydesign.com for more information.

There may also be government funding for certain crime reduction measures. Retailers in recognised deprived areas, for example, can qualify for grants to help with security improvements. Local authorities and crime prevention officers will tell you more.

ELECTRONIC CRIME

The most common crime reported by businesses completing the BCC survey in 2001 was not theft or arson, but internet crime – the loss of data, or of online services, as a result of computer viruses and attempts to hack into corporate websites.

These attacks are rarely fatal for a business, but clogged servers interrupt day-to-day trade. A company will suffer huge embarrassment and lost reputation if its website is taken over by someone else.

More businesses are switching over to broadband internet connections. These 'always on' services are faster but increase the risk of a third party gaining access to your systems through the new connection.

Protection starts with the basics:

- *Install a firewall – either software or a dedicated piece of hardware that checks the kind of information that is coming back down the line to your computers. It will block certain types of data, according to your pre-set criteria.*
- *Always use anti-virus software. This scans incoming email and files loaded from disk to try and weed out suspicious code that may be harmful to your systems.*
- *Update both anti-virus software and firewalls regularly. Threats evolve daily and, in the electronic world, you are only 100 per cent secure if you are up to date.*
- *Educate and train your staff. Warn them what to look out for in emails and how to spot suspicious attachments. And set out clear rules for who is permitted to load software onto your systems. With the growing use of PCs at home, some staff may unwittingly bring in problem software from home.*

THE INSIDE JOB

Employee crime is another serious risk to business. Very few employees have the power to do a Nick Leeson and bring a firm to its knees from the inside, but petty theft by staff is a constant drain on turnover, and many attacks on organisations are made by former employees with a grudge.

Studies by police have found, unsurprisingly, that businesses with large amounts of stock and poor record-keeping and accounts reconciliation are most prone to staff theft.

Many employers are willing to turn a blind-eye to some thefts for fear of damaging staff morale with 'heavy-handed' checks. However, once a culture of theft is established, it can become seen as a perk of the job. So, for the employer, prevention is better than cure.

Suggested actions for directors include:

- *Having a formal system that records who holds, and can issue, keys to the buildings.*
- *Vetting contract guarding companies and/or directly employed security staff fully – you want gamekeepers, not poachers.*
- *Where security passes or coded entry systems are used, ensuring passes are recovered from employees who leave and that codes are regularly changed.*
- *Setting out clearly the penalties for staff theft. Can anyone leave your premises at anytime, without fear of being checked?*

WORKING TOGETHER

Some of the most effective ways to reduce the threat of crime involve a firm working with others – either joining forces with agencies such as the police and local authorities or teaming up with several other businesses.

Examples of successful local anti-crime initiatives include a group of businesses on a North Derbyshire industrial estate clubbing together to share the costs of improved lighting, installation of CCTV, guarding services and security patrols; or shops in several town centres sharing the cost of bollards installed to reduce the risk of ram raids.

Some of the most interesting moves have come in the form of specific partnerships set up to reduce business crime, such as Business Crime Direct on Merseyside. This is part-funded by the Home Office and brings together local authorities, the police, Chambers of Commerce and small businesses.

The service provides free security advice for firms of up to 50 employees and contributes to the cost of recommended security improvements. The collective approach also makes it easier to collect data on business crime and to negotiate bigger improvements, such as new street lighting.

Business Crime Direct provides an excellent practical guide to reducing crime risk, available to anyone from its website www.businesscrimedirect.org.uk free of charge.

Chapter 9

Keeping control of cashflow

Poor payers can threaten the survival of your business. Chris Wheal, business journalist, suggests ways in which firms can keep their credit risks firmly under control

EXECUTIVE SUMMARY

- Cashflow and credit problems are the single biggest cause of business failure.
- Sound management policies can identify risks in advance and speed payments by customers.
- Invoice factoring and credit insurance provide a final safety net may suit some businesses.

The risks of poor credit management have never been greater. A staggering 43,458 companies went under last year, a rise of 7.2 per cent on 2001. The biggest single reason for business failure was poor cashflow – not getting paid in time to pay your own bills. That puts more companies out of business than bad debts, the second most common reason for businesses failing.

The late payment legislation, which has been phased in since 1998, was toughened last year to add fixed penalties of between £40 and £100 to each late-paid debt. But, despite this, the evidence suggests things are getting worse.

According to the Credit Management Research Centre (CMRC) at Leeds University Business School, 52 per cent of all invoices were paid late in 1996, but by 2002 that figure had risen to 56 per cent. Late payment by central government has worsened by ten per cent since 1998 and tardiness by overseas customers has increased by 15 per cent.

Large firms and overseas customers remain the most likely to pay late. But in the second quarter of 2002, small firms were feeling the squeeze so badly that late payment by this sector hit an all-time high, with 43 per cent paying bills late.

The best way to tackle credit risk is to identify it before you even start trading with a firm. Credit checking potential customers before making a sale is a must. Companies such as D&B (formerly Dun & Bradstreet) and ICC can provide credit reports for between £10 and £35 per company. Extra payments buy monitoring reports for each company throughout the year.

D&B can also identify the best potential customers for you in any given area, enabling you to target your sales staff at the firms with which you would be happy to trade.

KEEPING YOUR EAR TO THE GROUND

But there are other methods. Your competitors will have their views and your trade body may well keep a record of the good, the bad and the frankly too ugly to deal with. Also watch out for good news, such as a massive new order or a sudden increase in business from one of your clients. This could signal that another supplier has ceased supplying them because they have failed to pay their bills.

Even steady, solid customers need a watchful eye because 80 per cent of bad debt comes from existing customers, not new ones. The Institute of Credit Management recommends checking up on customers at least twice a year. With the high-profile corporate collapses that have seen household names become skeletons of their former selves, the importance of this cannot be over-stated.

D&B's senior analyst Philip Mellor points out that half of all companies fail within their first four years, so young businesses need extra attention. He says companies whose directors are in their thirties are five times more likely to go under than companies whose directors are in their fifties. And even if the company you're dealing with seems OK, check out the directors' other companies.

Once you've decided to do business with a particular firm, another risk that needs to be avoided is confusion over exactly what the terms of the contract are. Sales staff should make these

RAPID RESPONSE RATES

Canny credit management has helped Total Glass, in Kirby, Liverpool grow its turnover eight-fold over the past decade

The company, which supplies glass and windows to the building trade, employs more than 80 people, including a full-time account manager to ensure the cash keeps flowing.

One of the biggest changes in recent years has been the speed and information of credit reports. Total Glass uses ICC for its limited company reports, for example, and accesses them via the internet.

Don Mackenzie, account manager and a fellow of the Institute of Credit Management, says: "You get an answer back in seconds and it contains more information than ever before. I remember when you hand wrote letters to the bank and had to wait for a reply. It took seven days to open a new customer account and it now takes 20 minutes."

Previously every Total Glass customer was given 30-day terms, regardless. Now, few are. The company has it own scoring system enabling it to offer a range of terms and credit limits to most new customers quickly. "We decided we didn't want everyone on 30-day accounts," says Mackenzie.

Terms range from cash to 14 days, with just a select few on 30 days. "And we have customers whose terms have gone from cash on delivery to 14 days as their businesses have grown. We use that as a selling point – that we will help you grow," he says. Every now and then a new customer doesn't fit into its system and Mackenzie may take up to an hour to decide on the terms.

Total Glass has a team on the telephone reminding companies about their invoices, faxing and posting out reminders and statements and, if need be, taking legal action. "Our legal work is done inhouse," he explains. "My training as part of the institute means I can do it and that has saved our company a huge amount."

plain if you have standard terms, or be negotiating and agreeing them up front if you offer different terms to different customers. They should do this before signing the deal. Furthermore, you should always put your terms in writing so there can be no misunderstanding afterwards about how much and how quickly you were expecting to be paid.

LATE PAYMENT LEGISLATION

With the added strength of the late payment legislation, all businesses should be making clear in their terms that they will use the legislation to claim their rightful interest. However, currently only 38 per cent of businesses are making clear their rights under the legislation in their terms of trade, and in the SME sector it is down to just 15 per cent. Professor Nicholas Wilson of the CMRC says that stating that you will enforce your legal right to penalty interest and charges acts as a deterrent to late payers.

But for it to be a real deterrent you will need to use the legislation. Before the 1998 Act 17 per cent of companies included a contractual right to legislation in their terms but only one per cent of companies ever used it. By the turn of this year about seven per cent of companies were claiming interest from tardy payers. With the charges now in addition to the penalty interest, most credit experts expect that figure to rise.

The Better Payments Practice Group (BPPG) provides an online late payment interest calculator. It also suggests practical management techniques that can help you speed payment and control credit. Tips include:

- *Getting a signed delivery note for goods supplied and checking that the customer is satisfied with the quality and number delivered. Errors or faults are often used as an excuse for delaying payment.*
- *Always invoicing on time, accurately and to the correct person responsible in the format they require, using purchase order numbers or any other references necessary. This removes any excuse for late payment.*
- *Chasing up within a few days to ensure the invoice has been received, is in the correct format and is being processed.*
- *Chasing up the invoice a few days ahead of the due date or a few days ahead of the company's cheque run.*
- *Checking the status of each account before dispatching goods. Stop supply if the account is overdue. Set special terms*

(seven or 14 days) if the customer has paid late before; if the customer fails to meet the special terms, revert to pro-forma invoicing/cash on delivery – or stop supplying altogether.

- *Taking action to collect debts and using the legal tools at your disposal, including the late payment legislation, to claim interest and charges.*

If a customer does start paying late, don't let it drift. The BPPG suggests setting shorter terms immediately and, if the company fails to meet those, reverting to cash on delivery or ceasing supplying. Richard Wilson, business policy executive with the Institute of Directors and a member of the BPPG, says although small firms sometimes feel the big customer can simply go elsewhere, often the customer needs its supplier just as much. He also suggests that exposing the late payment in the media, even in local papers, can be a fillip to prompt payment in the future.

FACTORING AND INVOICE DISCOUNTING

If all this credit management sounds too much of a diversion from your core business, then factoring or invoice discounting may be an option. In simple terms these firms provide as much as 85 per cent of your invoice values to you immediately and, for a fee, do all credit checking, chasing and debt collecting on your behalf. You will need to have a turnover of at least £100,000 to interest a factoring firm.

No matter how you collect your money, if one big client going bust and not paying could put you out of business, you need to consider insuring against that risk. Factoring firms can buy that cover for or you can get it through your insurance broker. Coface, Gerling NCM and Euler Trade Indemnity are the three major companies that specialise in credit insurance for UK and international clients. You can insure your whole book of business for less than one per cent of turnover. Alternatively, cover just export business or even spotlight specific customers – but they will have to be good risk customers. Also, remember that insurers may refuse to cover some of your customers.

Chapter 10

Demystifying risk analysis

How can directors quantify the dangers facing their own business? Joe Aspey, managing director of Risk Analysis Services, offers some answers

EXECUTIVE SUMMARY

- Risks can be analysed in a logical and structured way.
- Companies need to set themselves thresholds of financial pain. This gives directors a clear warning light for when risks become dangerous and need to be managed or insured properly.
- This analysis will equip directors with a tasklist of priority actions.
- New projects, ventures and products bring new dangers to a business. They need a risk analysis too.

Business cannot operate without risk but directors can choose the level of risk they and their business carry. Commercial success needs to be balanced against this approach to risk.

Embarking on a business venture with no prior thought to risk leaves a company fundamentally vulnerable. Similarly, setting a programme for risk management without prior risk analysis or assessment may cause managers to miss, underestimate or deal with those threats ineffectively.

ORGANISING AN APPROACH TO RISK ANALYSIS

Let us demystify this subject and break it down into components that can apply to any business. A useful definition of risk is 'potential for downside, setback or failure'. If risk analysis is viewed as the process of identifying and evaluating risk, you can unpeel the layers and decide on containment strategies.

If tackling this subject for the first time, directors need a framework to help their decision-making. The goal is to:

- *identify risk;*
- *understand its nature;*
- *evaluate its potential;*
- *decide on appropriate action.*

The analysis will prompt firms to change strategy or to eliminate, control or insure a risk. Elimination may be difficult but practical management can reduce both severity and probability of an event. Directors should focus on the severity when deciding whether or not to insure a risk. If they are pro-active in managing insured risks, they will expect insurers to reflect this in their pricing.

METHODS OF IDENTIFYING AND ANALYSING RISK

Start by listing events or subject areas for detailed scrutiny. Take a thorough and broad approach. Here are some options:

- Shared brainstorming
  Throwing ideas onto a page is a good starting point. Do this first and seek as many viewpoints as possible. Ask your team to list risks and put them in priority order or give them a high, medium or low rating.
- Category headings
  On the opposite page is a table, with four headings that look at the business as a whole with a few examples for each one.
- Checklists
  These add an outside opinion and help you avoid serious gaps.
- SWOT and PEST analysis
  These can help to identify strategic issues. A PEST analysis examines political, economic, social and technological threats to highlight whether a business is in tune with its trading environment. Is the company becoming marginalised or is it slipping behind with technology or communication methods?

CATEGORY HEADINGS			
STRATEGY		OPERATIONS AND COMPLIANCE	
Competitors Demand cycles Changing markets Politics		Statutes and regulators Accounting controls Systems Recruitment	
FINANCIAL RISKS		HAZARDS	
Credit Currency Interest rate fluctuation Cashflow		Natural disasters Crime IT failure Loss of reputation	

- **Expert guidance**
  Risk managers, brokers and insurers have a wealth of experience and some offer specific risk analysis services. It is hard to take an objective view of your own business, so input from an expert may save time and money in the long run.

Once you have a reliable list, explore the 'downside' potential of each item to deteriorate before giving it a rating. Could an event or problem go beyond an obvious immediate cost and have a longer-term impact on a company's culture or revenue stream? Could it even interrupt the firm's ability to trade?

Next it is possible to rate each risk for severity and probability to produce a combined impact score.

KNOWING OUR PAIN THRESHOLDS

To support these ratings directors need financial benchmarks against which to judge severity. Whether the impact is instant or protracted, the end result will always be financial loss; and, whatever the cause, companies usually go out of business because they run out of cash.

So directors must define some pain thresholds to help them prioritise risks that can be managed and identify those that can be left to insurance.

Pain thresholds can be split into four levels, though the actual value of loss in each will vary from business to business.

The following example is based on a two-year-old company turning over £2m.

- **Level 1: No problem**
  Up to this figure, the firm could write out a cheque with minimal impact on cash, borrowing capacity or profit levels. In this example, say this is from £0-£10k.

- **Level 2: This would hurt**
  The firm would survive but would be more vulnerable and its ability to re-invest and grow would be weakened unless the directors could re-finance. In the same example, this might be from £10k-£50k.

- **Level 3: Potentially terminal**
  At this level, the business is severely weakened and unable to absorb further pain. Recovery would be in doubt and directors would risk losing control of their destiny. Perhaps this is from £50k-£100k.

- **Level 4: Instant collapse**
  In our example this is anything above £100k.

WORKING THROUGH A SAMPLE RISK ANALYSIS

Here is an analysis of a few risk issues using these financial pain thresholds to rate severity of an event from 1-4, and managers' judgement to rate probability of an event from 1-3. The two scores are multiplied to produce a combined score. In this case, the directors' parameters for action are to control everything with a combined score of 3 or more, and insure everything with a severity score of 2 or more. The scores can also be used to organise priorities, but managers must take full account of legal requirements whatever rating a risk scores.

EVENT	RISK			ACTION		
	Severity	Probability	Combined	Eliminate	Control	Insure
Bad debt	2	2	4		X	X
Fire	4	2	8		X	X
IT failure	3	3	9		X	X
Libel action	1	1	1			
Cash theft	1	3	3	X		

RESULTS OF EVALUATION

So let us now assess what this evaluation tells us.

Bad debt

The initial severity rating was raised from 1 to 2 on realising that a bad debt could be accompanied by future loss of revenue in a period when customers are hard to win. The firm could also be left with redundant stock so the first assessment of a £10,000 loss was revised to a total of £25,000.

Fire

This is the big destroyer so the business obviously has fire cover. Management thinks the risk is low but they must assume the probability is at least 2 until they have carried out a detailed assessment. Even though this does not attract the highest combined score, a Fire Risk Assessment is a legal requirement so it must be a top priority item.

IT failure

The impact of an IT failure is hard to quantify but, make no mistake, this is a serious issue since it only takes a computer virus to interrupt trading. Achieving the highest score demands a complete review of IT security, back up and support and an investigation of the insurance options.

Libel action

A low risk issue. This business publishes no 'sensitive' material and has tight rules about what people can say in company emails. Directors will keep this under review but it is a low scoring item and demands no action based on our parameters.

Cash theft

The practice of holding cash for petty expenses is an invitation to thieves and, once they find cash on the premises, they will be back for more with all the attendant damage and disruption. By setting up supplier accounts and maximising use of company credit cards, directors can eliminate this risk completely.

PROJECTS ARE INHERENTLY RISKY

History is littered with projects that failed through bad judgement, over-optimism or lack of planning. Tales of military blunders, and inventions that never reach the market abound, and so it is, potentially, with all projects.

Any decision to launch a new product, enter new markets or undertake a construction contract is accompanied by heavy downside potential. If directors are not realistic, they may underestimate development time and exhaust a company's cash before reaching the market. They may misunderstand the market or the best route to it and, if a product is launched without sufficient development, the business may suffer the expense and knock-on effect of a service suspension or product recall.

Site work may introduce safety and environmental concerns with increased potential for prosecution. Logistical or labour issues could delay a project or take costs dangerously over budget.

These dangers make it clear that success of a new project may depend heavily on the quality of a risk analysis prior to commitment.

Whether a business is small or large, the journey will be safer if entrepreneurial spirit is tempered with realism and awareness.

Chapter 11

Falling back on best laid plans

Despite the best planning and most careful risk analysis, accidents will still happen. This is when a properly constructed business continuity plan can be priceless, says Peter Viner, managing director of Ark First

EXECUTIVE SUMMARY

- Business continuity planning is about keeping a company going through the worst fate can throw at it.
- A business continuity plan is a blueprint for what needs to be done, both on the day of a crisis and in the immediate aftermath.
- Continuity plans keep a company focused on its objectives. They are not about recreating what is lost.

A business can take years to develop its client base, reputation and the brand on which it trades. Yet it can take only a few days or weeks for a badly-handled serious incident to destroy that reputation and lose a business its client base.

Consciously or sub-consciously, many of us assume we're immune to risk – that 'it will never happen to me' – or that insurance will take care of us.

Insurance can provide some financial assistance, but it can't recover lost clients whose orders have not been filled due to a sudden crisis, nor restore a damaged reputation or brand.

Business continuity management (BCM) is a process designed with one thing in mind: helping businesses survive a sudden shock. Its principles are simple and applicable to all businesses, no matter what their size or makeup.

Done correctly, BCM is an ongoing and embedded process in the business. It embraces the central theme of risk management, that prevention is better than cure. But BCM recognises that it is impractical and impossible to remove or reduce all risks and that accidents and disasters will strike a business from causes and in ways that it may not have envisaged.

Good continuity management will give a business a sound strategy and a practical set of instructions that staff can follow to try to keep a company on its feet.

THE NEXT STEP FROM RISK ASSESSMENT

Continuity management follows on naturally from the process of risk assessment described in the previous chapter. This risk analysis will give directors an awareness of the key threats their business faces. It will highlight those risks that can be mitigated easily, those which need to be contained and flag up those that can never be completely managed.

If a risk analysis has been done thoroughly, a company will have a clear understanding of its critical structures, resources, and of its appetite for risk – those financial pain thresholds described previously. This is the starting point for the building the business continuity plan (BCP) itself.

This plan should provide key executives with a framework and reference guide that will enable them to make the most appropriate decisions when dealing with a crisis or disastrous event. The aim is to minimise disruption or damage to the business to enable the business to fulfil its objectives.

The linkage to business objectives is key: companies sometimes come unstuck because they think business continuity is about putting everything back as it was. In fact, handled correctly, a major incident may be a chance for the company to implement dramatic changes to its operations and its processes, consistent with achieving the business objectives more efficiently.

GETTING EMPLOYEE BUY-IN

A key element of successful business continuity management is that those involved have an understanding of what needs to be achieved. Board members, senior management and those managing and maintaining survival plans should be provided with reference material on the operation, objectives and practical application of the process.

In the meantime, the rest of the staff will require a basic awareness of the company's aims in following the BCM discipline. Employees should be guided on what risk is and how it may affect the business. A reporting structure for risk issues should be instituted. All should be made aware that their assistance is invaluable in identifying risks and helping management to implement changes.

SURVIVAL TEAMS

These are the people who will bring the business continuity process to life. In larger organisations it may be appropriate to appoint several survival teams with a head office team that will oversee the others.

These teams should be made up of individuals who have the requisite understanding of the business and its processes, are senior enough to make decisions, and are calm and capable of decision-making under stressful circumstances. A team's first responsibility is for overseeing the maintenance of the BCP and, secondly, for handling the crisis situation and the subsequent business recovery.

PLAN BUILDING

The business continuity plan should be designed to address the consequences of a risk, rather than the risk itself. The plan needs to be concise and logically laid out. Where applicable, it should refer to supporting documentation that will assist the survival teams in making decisions and carrying out actions.

Each plan will have its own strategy that will fit the business and its objectives. However, there are several generic elements to the structure of a good plan.

The BCP should contain an introduction, which sets out the scope of the document, the roles and responsibilities of the teams and those who form part of them.

The core document itself should be split into three main sections:

a) Crisis Management Plan (CMP)

The CMP is designed to cover the initial management of a potential crisis situation and will generally deal with actions and responses in the first 24-36 hours of an incident and its co-ordination. It is likely to cover areas such as: emergency call-out lists, evacuation procedures, location and access details for key information, employee and public safety procedures, incident investigation, impact assessment, incident containment, public relations and communications, hot-site invocation and escalation procedures for bringing into effect other elements of the plan.

A CMP is likely to be the most used portion of the plan, as a properly handled crisis situation does not necessarily turn into a disaster.

b) Business Continuity Plan (BCP)

This element of the plan is not concerned with what has happened or the restoration of the assets of the business, unless such actions help the business to continue in the most effective way.

The BCP focuses on enabling the business to continue trading until such time as it can be restored to normal operation. It is likely to cover areas such as: continued public relations and communications strategies, sub-contracting production, moving to temporary alternative sites, dealing with insurers, banks' and clients' expectations and legal issues, instigating backups, data recovery, and any actions that will assist the business in maintaining its clients, reputation, production or services in line with its objectives.

c) Restoration Plan (RP)

The RP deals primarily with the restoration and recovery of the resources of the business to a level where the business can resume normal operations in the shortest possible time.

This area of the plan may include such actions as appointing a disaster restoration company, salvage strategy, data recompilation, restoration of buildings and assets and infrastructure and all that is associated with this, such as recruiting replacement staff, dealing with insurers and loss adjusters, etc.

MAKE CONTINUITY PLANNING ONGOING

Business continuity planning needs to be embedded within the business ethos. It should be ongoing, adaptable and able to change with the company. The BCM process should be easy to maintain once the initial development and groundwork has been done on awareness, detailing the organisation and its resources, setting up survival teams and making provision for regular risk analysis.

Businesses that instigate the BCM process not only make themselves more resilient, they make themselves more attractive to insurers by showing a pro-active attitude to risk. Insurers recognise that businesses that practice BCM have reduced the potential likelihood, frequency and severity of any claims and thus may provide preferential terms or coverage to that business.

Businesses that want to learn more about BCM can refer to their insurers, whose experience enables them to give valuable advice to their policyholders. Alternatively, the internet has links to a huge number of companies offering BCM products, consultancy and training services, including Ark First at www.arkfirst.com

Chapter 12

Preparing for the risks of the future

In an ever-changing world, directors need to be alert to new dangers, says George Cameron, a director of the Institute of Risk Management and principal consultant at Thomas Miller Risk Management

EXECUTIVE SUMMARY

- Entirely new risks will present new challenges. Directors cannot ignore them.
- Assessing new risks may be difficult, but it is better to consider all risks credible, especially where the public could be affected.
- Directors must consider their personal liability, even in voluntary roles.
- The risk management standard gives a framework to assess and control emerging risks.

Businesses are dynamic. They cannot and do not stand still, changing to adapt to the new demands of customers, requirements of legislatures or whims of society. As the world continues to evolve so does the business climate. The successful entrepreneur, director or manager is the one that anticipates needs or events and positions the business to take advantage of, meet or deflect the challenge.

IMPACT OF 2001 IN RISK PLANNING

The year 2001 proved that, whatever else, some risks cannot be foreseen. The events of September 11 are burned on everyone's minds and demonstrate a new state of terrorist activity not previously conceived of.

In the UK, where we have lived with the consequences of terrorism for a very long period, most terrorist organisations tended to have accepted that killing or injuring the public was counterproductive. Although substantial property damage and interruption to economic activity could be anticipated, contingency plans were drawn up on the basis of staff being able to move to alternative centres and recommence business. September 11 introduced a grim new concept into such planning; not only do you need alternative sites but also back-up staff to man these locations. Future contingency plans must build in this requirement.

In addition, directors will be faced by the insurance market's decision to restrict terrorism cover. While cover will be available at an additional cost, the restrictions likely to be imposed by insurers will be considerable. The extension of terrorism action to hit random commercial targets will require directors to think carefully about their businesses. Although the physical terrorism threat to their own staff and property may be minimal, directors should evaluate the potential effects were a supplier or customer affected by terrorism action. The current reliance on 'just in time' stocking, outsourcing and external services – a trend which is likely to grow – could have major effects on a business in the event of the supplier or customer being affected by a terrorism incident.

THE 'BLAME' AND 'COMPENSATION' CULTURES

A further trend in Europe is the increasing 'blame' culture, under which public opinion demands that a 'culprit' be found for any incident involving death or injury. There is an increasing trend to demand a scapegoat, evidenced by the current government's determination to legislate on corporate killing and to make directors personally liable to penalties.

This culture, when combined with the increasing propensity to seek compensation when 'blame' is allocated, is creating a regime of uncertainty that makes it difficult for insurers to provide meaningful protection for directors at a reasonable price.

The uncertainty is enhanced by the redrawing of legal boundaries on blame. For example, on the Fairchild case, the House of Lords has decided that an injured party can pursue one past employer in respect of mesothelioma, leaving other potential defendants to allocate responsibility amongst themselves.

In the USA, courts have redrawn the boundaries of who can claim, allowing those in fear of asbestosis, including family members who could have been peripherally exposed, to lodge claims for fear of contamination. And with the USA authorities now threatening directors with imprisonment for wrongful accounting declarations, again, individuals have to consider carefully the implications for doing business overseas or taking on a new role.

FUTURE LIABILITY THREATS

The problem of asbestos has been in the public domain for a very long time. What might be the next big health and liability threat for businesses? Concerns exist over toxic mould and Artex in buildings, but these exposures do not appear to be on the same scale as asbestos.

There is also substantial public fear about the effects of electro-magnetic fields, either emanating from power lines or, more currently, mobile phones and their relay stations. Despite considerable investigations over an extended period, no exposure has been proved in respect of power lines and the alarmist predictions made regarding mobile telephones have not produced the number of injuries predicted. As chapter 3 highlighted, environmental damage and pollution has moved much higher up the business agenda, with a raft of new legislation.

Whether these emerging risks are real or imagined, directors must consider them in their risk assessments. Even if the experts think a supposed risk will have little or no impact, the directors may have to show a higher standard of care in the light of press comment and public perceptions at the time of the assessment.

REVISED ATTITUDES OF INSURERS

Changing weather patterns also present a real risk. Insurers have shown a trend to treat damage due to storm and flood perils as ‘inevitable’, removing cover for them from their policies in some areas of the country. This poses a challenge for businesses in risk areas, which will not only face losing insurance against physical damage, but also the business interruption cover that follows.

It is conceivable that if neither government nor insurers can provide the right safety net, business will either close in certain areas or band together to form co-operatives to create their own flood defence and compensation schemes. This is how companies reacted to the threat of fire three centuries ago and it may be that history has to repeat itself.

THREAT OF DISQUALIFICATION

Directors also face a new level of vulnerability as a result of the ongoing drive to implement corporate governance at all levels of society, including voluntary bodies. Many directors, because of their particular skills, have additional appointments including:

- *non-executive directorships on the boards of other companies;*
- *as trustees of charities or pensions funds;*
- *public appointments, such as school governors or members of local health trusts.*

A failure by any of these bodies to implement good corporate governance practices could lead to a finding of culpability and, possibly, disqualification of a director. Whenever such appointments are accepted, directors should ensure that adequate corporate governance systems are implemented for any such organisation. (See chapter 6 for more on directors' disqualification.)

THE RISK MANAGEMENT STANDARD

While there are a tremendous number of risks that directors are required to assess – some requiring 20–20 hindsight – potential solutions are being developed. In 2002, the Institute of Risk Management along, with others, launched the Risk Management Standard.

This provides a practical framework within which risk assessments can be carried out and a coherent process, organisation and structure for the implementation of risk management can be established (see panel on page 76). Early indications are that the standard has been well received.

FRAMEWORK FOR SUCCESS

The new Risk Management Standard is a collaboration between the UK's three main risk management groups, the Institute of Risk Management (IRM), the Association of Insurance and Risk Managers and Alarm – the national forum for public sector risk managers

The Standard sets out a framework that directors and managers can use to monitor risk in their organisations. It highlights best practice and the terminology of risk control and should help companies to create a risk culture that allows them to recognise risk and make the right management decisions at the right time. It is designed to be flexible enough to be of value to organisations large and small.

Copies of the Standard can be downloaded from the IRM website at www.theirm.org free of charge.

Adopting and implementing the Risk Management Standard, which assists in evaluating positive aspects of risk as well as its adverse consequences, will enable directors to prove that they have robust processes in place to evaluate and deal with risk.

Trade and professional bodies

Alarm – The National Forum for Risk Management in the Public Sector
ALARM, Queens Drive, Exmouth, EX8 2AY
Tel: 01395 223399; www.alarm-uk.com

Association of British Insurers
51, Gresham Street, London, EC2V 7HQ
Tel: 020 7600 3333; www.abi.org.uk

Association of Insurance and Risk Managers
AIRMIC Secretariat, 6 Lloyd's Avenue, London, EC3N 3AX
Tel: 020 7480 7610; www.airmic.com

Association of Occupational Health Nurse Practitioners
PO Box 11785, Peterhead, AB42 5YG
Tel: 0845 225 5937; www.aohnp.co.uk

British Insurance Brokers' Association
14 Bevis Marks, London EC3A 7NT.
Tel: 020 7623 9043; www.biba.org.uk

Chartered Institute of Personnel and Development
CIPD House, Camp Road, Wimbledon, London, SW19 4UX
Tel: 020 8971 9000; www.cipd.co.uk

Factors & Discounters Association
Boston House, The Little Green Richmond, Surrey, TW9 1QE
Tel: 020 8332 9955; www.factors.org.uk

The Institute of Credit Management
The Water Mill, Station Road, South Luffenham, Leicestershire, LE15 8NB
Tel: 01780 722900; www.icm.org.uk

The Institute of Risk Management
Lloyd's Avenue House, 6 Lloyd's Avenue, London EC3N 3AX
Tel 020 7709 9808; www.theirm.org

Royal College of Nursing
20 Cavendish Square, London, W1G 0RN
Tel: 020 7409 3333; www.rcn.org.uk

Other useful information sources
Fire prevention

Fire Protection Association
UK-wide fire safety organisation. Source of expert advice and help on all aspects of fire safety. Welcomes corporate members.
Bastille Court, 2 Paris Garden, London SE1 8ND
Tel: 020 7902 5300; www.thefpa.co.uk

British Automatic Sprinkler Association
Group for specialist providers of sprinkler and fire prevention equipment.
Richmond House, Broad Street, Ely CB7 4AH
Tel 01353 659187; www.basa.org.uk/

Health and Safety

Health and Safety Executive
The UK Health and Safety Commission (HSC) and the Health and Safety Executive (HSE) are responsible for the regulation of almost all the risks to health and safety arising from work activity in Britain. They operate via a network of local offices, helplines, publications and through a comprehensive website www.hse.gov.uk

There are a wide variety of advice and information services under the HSE umbrella. The most useful for directors includes the publication 'Directors' responsibilities for health and safety', which is available at www.hse.gov.uk/pubns/indg343.pdf and the free advice on health and safety. This is available from HSE InfoLine, tel: 08701 545500, email: hseinformationservices@natbrit.com. Alternatively, write to HSE Information Services, Caerphilly Business Park, Caerphilly, CF83 3GG

www.hsedirect.com has an online archive of all the HSE publications, plus the detailed legislation. This is a commercial site, so access is charged.

www.coshh-essentials.org.uk has details on the Control of Substances Hazardous to Health regulations. Try the downloadable booklet 'A brief guide to COSHH' as a start.

DTI Work-Life Balance campaign
Details for employers on helping their staff to manage work and home life more effectively, including information on grants available for employers who introduce flexible working strategies.
www.dti.gov.uk/work-lifebalance/index.html

Repetitive Strain Injury Association
Charity focused on advice on the causes and treatment of workplace RSI-type injuries. Includes specific risk management advice.
380-384 Harrow Road, London W9 2HU
Tel: 020 7266 2000; www.rsi.org.uk

Royal Society for the Prevention of Accidents
Works towards accident reduction in all facets of life, including the workplace. A provider of health and safety advice, training and consultancy.
Edgbaston Park, 353 Bristol Road, Edgbaston, Birmingham B5 7ST, UK
Tel: 0121 248 2000; www.rospa.co.uk

UK National Work-Stress Network
Workplace stress campaign group, with newsletters and information factsheets on managing stress at work.

Brian Robinson (Network Coordinator) 9 George Drive, Drayton, Norwich, Norfolk NR8 6ED
Tel:01603 868249; www.workstress.net

Legal information

UK legislation: The Stationery Office, PO Box 276 London SW8 5DT
Tel: 0870 600 5522; www.legislation.hmso.gov.uk

EU legislation: The Official Journal, Stationery Office, International Sales Agency, 51 Nine Elms Lane, London SW8 50R
Tel: 020 7873 8787

The Forensic Insolvency Recovery Service (FIRS): Nick Miller (tel: 020 7566 4020 or Tim Bramston (01727 896000)
www.insolvency.gov.uk/information/firs.htm

Crime prevention

Business Crime Direct

Regional anti-crime initiative working in Merseyside, but with useful advice for businesses nation-wide.
Liverpool Chamber of Commerce & Industry, 1 Old Hall Street, Liverpool L3 9HG. Tel: 0151 227 1234; www.businesscrimedirect.org.uk

Arson Prevention Bureau

Joint venture between Home Office and Association of British Insurers to combat Arson. Source of specialist risk management advice.
51 Gresham Street, London EC2V 7HQ
Tel: 020 7216 7474; www.arsonpreventionbureau.org.uk

www.crimereduction.gov.uk

Central Government advice and information site on a wide range of crime reduction issues. It has basic information for all businesses and links to other organisations. The site also contains a more in-depth Crime Reduction Toolkit, aimed at retailers and small businesses.

Secured by Design

Police-driven service to improve security of property at the design stage.
ACPO Crime Prevention Initiatives, 25 Victoria Street, London SW1H 0EX.
Tel: 0207 227 3423 E-mail: acpocpi@acpo.pnn.police.uk

Credit management

Better Payments Practice Group www.payontime.co.uk
Free guides which can be downloaded from this site include 'A User's Guide to the amended late payment legislation' and 'The BPPG guide to getting paid on time'.

Environmental issues

The Environment Agency

Covers England and Wales and operates through a network of regional offices. Enforces environmental and anti-pollution laws and can advise firms. For details of your local office call 0845 9333111 or log onto the website www.environment-agency.gov.uk

Scottish Environment Protection Agency

Mirrors the activities of the Environment Agency in Scotland.
Erskine Court, Castle Business Park, Stirling, FK9 4TR
Tel: 01786 457700; www.sepa.org.uk

NetRegs

This excellent website allows users to examine their business stage by stage, to check what, if any, environmental rules apply to their operations.
www.environment-agency.gov.uk/netregs

Workplace issues

The TUC

Digests of health & safety and employment law from union and employee perspective, but some useful information for managers too. Facility to sign up to e-mail alterts on health and safety issues.
Congress House, Great Russell Street, London WC1B 3LS
Tel: 020 7636 4030; www.tuc.org.uk

The Work Foundation

Independent think tank and consultancy on workplace issues. Useful info on employment law, corporate governance and health and safety.
Peter Runge House, 3 Carlton House Terrace, London SW1Y 5DG
Tel: 0870 165 6700; www.theworkfoundation.com

Risk management and business continuity

www.axa4business.co.uk
Internet information service run by Axa Insurance for small businesses, including risk management help and advice on a wide range of business topics.

Business Continuity Institute

Group promoting good practice in business continuity management and disaster recovery.
Offers free guides and factsheets, sets professional standards and endorses training programmes.
PO Box 4474, Worcester WR6 5YA
Tel: 0870 603 8783; www.thebci.org